AD 43

The Roman conquest begins

AD 61

Rebellion of Boudicca crushed

AD 401–409

Roman armies leave Britain

C AD 430s

Angles, Saxons, Jutes and Frisians begin to settle in Britain

C AD 500

Scots, from Ireland, settle in north west Britain

AD 793

First Viking raid, on the monastery at Lindisfarne

AD 843

Kenneth MacAlpin becomes first king to rule over both Picts and Scots. The beginning of Scotland.

AD 1016

Cnut of Denmark becomes King of England

AD 1066

Normans defeat and kill the last Anglo-Saxon king at Hastings

The Celts

Two thousand years ago, Britain was the home of the ancient Britons, or Celts. The Celts, who also lived across much of Europe, were a mixture of different peoples. In Britain, for example, there were small dark Celts as well as tall sandy-haired ones. What made them Celts was their shared way of life. They spoke a Celtic language which was like Welsh. They worshipped Celtic gods and dressed in a Celtic style.

Powerful nobles

The Celts belonged to many tribes ruled by kings and queens. There was a small class of powerful nobles, who showed off their wealth by wearing expensive ornaments of gold, silver and bronze. These nobles ruled over a much larger class of farmers and slaves, who grew the food. There were also skilled metalworkers, who made the weapons, tools and jewellery.

This mirror belonged to a Celtic noblewoman. This is the back, decorated with swirling patterns. The other side was polished until it reflected its owner's face.

Rich men wore a torc, a neck-ring made of twisted gold or silver.

Round houses

The Celts lived in small farming settlements scattered throughout the countryside. Their houses were round, with tall sloping thatched roofs to keep the rain off. Although these houses vanished long ago, they sometimes leave marks, such as post-holes in the ground, showing how they were built.

This is a reconstruction of a Celtic house, built at Butser Hill in Hampshire.

Gods – did they live in water?

Celts worshipped dozens of different gods. They offered the gods sacrifices – gifts, such as precious metalwork. They threw these gifts into rivers, pools and holy springs – places where the gods were thought to live. People were also killed as sacrifices to the gods. The sacrifices were believed to please the gods. In return, the gods would protect the people.

Religion was controlled by priests, called druids. They performed the sacrifices and they were also thought to be able to see into the future.

Treasure from a bog

In 1943, more than 100 pieces of Celtic metalwork were found in a bog on Anglesey, Wales. There were swords, shields, jewellery, chariot fittings and a chain, worn by slaves. These had been thrown into the bog, then a lake, as gifts for the gods.

Celtic warriors

The Celtic tribes were always fighting each other. They went to war to conquer land, to steal cattle, and to capture slaves. The warriors loved fighting, to win fame by showing their skill and bravery. Women also went into battle, to encourage their men with their shouts.

A beautifully decorated bronze horned helmet and shield. Both objects were found in the River Thames, perhaps thrown there as a sacrifice to the gods. Such armour was worn for show as much as for protection.

'They love to walk out in front of the battle-line to challenge the bravest of their enemies to single combat. And if someone accepts the challenge, they loudly shout about their own bravery. At the same time, they yell insults at their enemy, to rob him of his fighting spirit.'

A Greek writer, Diodorus of Sicily, describes the behaviour of Celts in battle

The warriors fought on foot, on horseback and from wooden chariots. Each light chariot was pulled by a pair of fast horses. The warriors drove them at great speed around the battlefield while hurling spears at their enemies. Then they leapt down to fight with long slashing swords. The richest warriors carried bronze shields and wore helmets, though many went into battle almost naked. It was more important to show bravery than to protect yourself with armour.

'When they leave the battlefield, they hang the heads of their enemies from the necks of their horses. When they have returned home, they nail these heads above the doors of their homes. They will proudly show the heads of famous enemies to strangers.'

Strabo, another Greek writer, wrote that Celts were 'head-hunters'

Hillforts

In the south and west of Britain, you can still see the earth banks of great hillforts, built by the Celts to defend themselves from their enemies. Wooden walls once stood at the top of the earth banks, and the area inside was full of round-houses. These hillforts were the strongholds of British kings and queens.

This is Maiden Castle, a huge Celtic hillfort in Dorset. Here you can see the entrance to the fort, defended by a maze of earth banks.

The coming of the Romans

While the British tribes were busy fighting each other, a great empire was conquering much of Europe to the south. The Romans, who ruled this empire, were different in almost every way from the Celts. They were much better organised, ruled by a single powerful government. They lived in cities linked up by well-built roads. Their armies were made up of highly-trained, full-time soldiers. Romans also believed that they had the right to conquer and rule other peoples.

'All the Britons dye their bodies blue with a plant called woad, which gives them a terrifying appearance. They wear their hair long, and shave the whole of their bodies except their head and upper lip.'

Julius Caesar describes the Celts of Britain

BRITAIN

German tribes

GAUL
(France)

SPAIN

ITALY

Rome

AFRICA

MEDITERRANEAN SEA

The Roman Empire c. 55 BC

Julius Caesar

In 55 and 54 BC, a Roman general called Julius Caesar led two expeditions to Britain. He defeated the tribes who fought against him, but did not try to conquer the island. His real aim was to impress people back in Rome. To them, Britain was a land at the end of the world. They were amazed that Caesar had even managed to visit such a far-away place.

To impress his fellow Romans, Caesar wrote a book in which he described his expeditions to Britain. A lot of what we know of ancient Britain comes from Caesar's book.

Roman soldiers cross a river on a bridge of boats. Unlike the Britons they wore plenty of protective armour.

The riches of Britain

After Caesar's expedition, there was new trade between Britain and the Roman Empire. Roman merchants sailed to Britain with cargoes of wine, olive oil and pottery. They exchanged these for grain, cattle, gold, silver, iron, tin, hunting dogs and slaves. Soon, some of the British rulers had a taste for Roman luxury goods. Meanwhile, the Romans realised that Britain might be a place worth conquering.

The Great Invasion

In AD 41, a man called Claudius became the new emperor, or ruler, of the Romans. He wanted to start his rule with a great military victory. This was the best way to make yourself popular with the Roman people. Claudius decided that the time had come to conquer Britain.

In AD 43, a huge Roman invading fleet, carrying 40 000 soldiers, landed in Kent. The soldiers marched inland and fought two battles against the Britons, who were led by King Caratacus. The Britons fought bravely, but they were beaten by the Roman soldiers, who were better trained.

Claudius arrives

Soon after, the emperor himself arrived in Britain with reinforcements. He also had trained elephants with him, to amaze and terrify the Britons. Several British kings came to Claudius to surrender. Some were happy to be ruled by the Romans. Others could see no hope of beating them, and they wanted to be on the winning side.

The army moves west

The Roman army now moved westwards, capturing the British hillforts, one after another. In one fort, archaeologists dug up the bodies of Britons who had died fighting the Romans.

This Briton had been killed by an iron arrowhead, fired from a Roman catapult.
You can see the arrowhead stuck in his backbone.

Caratacus captured

Caratacus fought the Romans for eight more years, leading raids from the mountains of Wales. When the Romans invaded Wales, he escaped north to the land of the Brigantes tribe (see map on page 16). He hoped to lead this tribe in a new war against Rome. But Queen Cartimandua of the Brigantes arrested Caratacus. To please the Romans, she handed Caratacus over to them.

Caratacus in Rome

Caratacus was taken to Rome and brought before the Emperor Claudius. The Emperor admired the British king and gave him a house in Rome. Caratacus was amazed at the size and wealth of the city.

'When you have all these riches, why did you want to take our poor huts from us?'

A question asked by Caratacus in Rome

'I had horses, men, arms, wealth. Are you surprised that I am sorry to lose them? If you want to rule the world, does it follow that everyone else should welcome becoming slaves?'

Caratacus told the Romans why he had fought against them for so long

A coin of King Caratacus, who led the Britons against the Romans.

Queen Boudicca

While the Roman army was still fighting against tribes in the west of Britain, the first towns were being built in the south east. One town, Colchester, was built by Roman soldiers. After 25 years' service, they retired from the army. They married local women, and settled down to live in Colchester. The eastern tribes, the Iceni and the Trinovantes, hated these new towns.

The burning of Colchester

In AD 60, Queen Boudicca of the Iceni led the eastern tribes in a surprise attack on the town. Soon the wooden buildings were in flames, and black smoke was rising into the sky. Everyone in Colchester was killed.

The final battle

With each success, more Britons came to join Boudicca. The Roman army, which marched from Wales to fight her, was greatly outnumbered. But the Romans were better soldiers. When the two forces finally met, somewhere in the Midlands, the Romans won a complete victory. Boudicca killed herself.

What did Boudicca look like?

Boudicca was described by a writer called Dio Cassius. He had never seen Boudicca. He described her as he imagined she must have looked. Like all Romans, he was shocked at the idea of a woman leading men into battle. Such a woman had to look terrifying.

'She was very tall and grim-looking, with a piercing gaze and a harsh voice. She had a mass of red hair which fell down to her hips. She looked terrifying.'

A writer called Dio Cassius described Boudicca

The rebels hated the Romans so much that they even smashed their tombstones in the Colchester cemetery. This stone (right) shows a cavalryman called Longinus trampling on a defeated Briton. His face had been smashed by the rebels before the stone was thrown to the ground.

After Colchester, the tribes attacked two other new towns, St Albans and London. These were also burned to the ground.

Winning over the Britons

For many British people, life was better under the Romans. Roman rule brought peace, ending the warfare between the tribes. Although people had to pay taxes to the Romans, the money was used to build new towns and a network of roads.

Amazing buildings

The Romans brought new building materials to Britain – concrete and brick. They also showed the Britons new ways of using the old materials, stone and wood. They cut stone into fine square blocks for grand public buildings. They also built timber-framed houses with more than one floor. For the first time, British homes had an upstairs.

The Britons must have been amazed when they saw the first Roman buildings going up. Even if they hated the Romans, they could only be impressed by the wonderful new buildings.

Luxury living

Rich Britons, who had previously lived in round-houses, now had the chance to live in luxury. Some built themselves grand country houses with their own baths and under-floor heating.

At Fishbourne in Sussex, the remains of a great Roman palace have been discovered. Its floors were covered in mosaics, beautiful pictures made out of thousands of tiny coloured tiles.

Mosaic artists loved inventing strange animals, like this winged sea-horse, from Fishbourne.

Fishbourne was built around AD 80. It may have been built for the local king, Cogidubnus, who helped the Romans during their invasion.

Cogidubnus welcomed Roman rule. He even took a new Roman name – Tiberius Claudius Cogidubnus.

Roads

The Roman soldiers built long straight roads, linking up the new towns of Britain. Roman roads were the best in the world. Unlike the old muddy tracks, they were paved, so they could be used even in the wettest weather.

Some roads built by the Roman soldiers are still used today. This one runs through London between Radlett and Borehamwood.

A bust from Bath, showing one of the new Roman hairstyles copied by British women.

A Roman education

The children of the richest Britons were given a Roman education. They were taught to speak the Roman language (Latin), and to read and write. They also began to dress like Romans. British women copied the hairstyles of the Roman empresses, whose portraits appeared on coins. Men stopped wearing loose trousers and gold neck torcs. Instead they wore a woollen tunic over bare legs.

Life in the towns

The Romans built the first real towns in Britain. Every town had straight streets of shops, workshops and houses. There was a council building, for local government, a law court, and a market place. There were also places to relax, such as a large public bath house. Roman Britons went to the baths to wash, exercise and meet their friends.

The market place

The market place was used by local farmers, who came to sell their crops. For the towns' craftworkers, it was a place to sell the things they made, such as pottery and woven cloth. You could also buy goods from abroad, such as olive oil, wine and spicy fish sauce.

Main forts

Main towns*
*(see below)

1	York	7	Gloucester
2	Lincoln	8	Bath
3	Leicester	9	Exeter
4	Colchester	10	Winchester
5	St Albans	11	London
6	Caerleon	12	Canterbury

—— **Major roads**

TAEZALI **Names of Celtic tribes**

N

Roman Britain

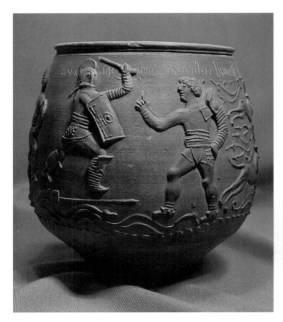

Gladiators fighting, on a vase from Colchester. The gladiator holding up his finger has lost the fight and is asking for mercy.

Entertainment

Roman towns often had theatres for plays, and amphitheatres (big oval buildings used for shows). The Romans loved watching fights to the death between slaves called gladiators. Wild animals, such as bears from Scotland, were also killed in the shows.

The gods of Roman Britain

The Romans banned human sacrifice, and they taught the Britons to worship new gods, such as Minerva, goddess of wisdom. However, they did not try to stop the worship of the Celtic gods. Honouring local gods helped the Romans win over the people they conquered. The Romans also believed that these gods were real. They wanted to get the British gods' power on their side.

Every town had temples where people could worship the gods. At Bath, there was a holy spring of warm water, where the Britons worshipped a goddess of healing, called Sulis. The Romans thought that Sulis sounded like their own goddess, Minerva. A new temple was built over the spring, dedicated to the goddess 'Sulis Minerva'.

A Roman curse

People came to the temple to ask favours of the goddess. They offered gifts to her, such as money and jewellery. They sent her messages, scratched on sheets of lead, which they threw into the spring. Some of these messages were curses (spells designed to harm an enemy). For example, one man asked the goddess to kill the thief who had stolen his hooded cloak.

A bust of Minerva, goddess of wisdom, found in Bath

Life on the frontiers

Roman Britain was like two different countries. Most of the towns and big country houses were in the low lying south and east. The Romans found the hilly north and west much harder to rule. This was the military area of Roman Britain, where the army lived in stone forts.

The Romans invaded Scotland several times over the years, building forts and roads there. But they were never able to hold their conquests for long.

Some of the biggest forts, such as Caerleon in Wales, had their own amphitheatres, where the soldiers could watch gladiators fight. This is what remains today.

Hadrian's Wall

In AD 122, the Emperor Hadrian built a 117 km-long wall across northern Britain. This was the frontier, defending Roman Britain from the northern tribes.

In AD 139, the Emperor Antoninus Pius invaded Scotland, and built another frontier wall, further north. This new wall crossed Scotland at its narrowest part. This made it seem a much better place to have the frontier. But the Romans could not control the northern tribes, and they soon abandoned their new wall. Once more, Hadrian's Wall was the frontier of Roman Britain.

A Roman fort

At regular spaces along the wall, there were eighty small forts and sixteen larger ones. Each of the big forts included a hospital, stables, grain stores, workshops and toilets. Outside the fort, there was a bath-house, where the men could go when they were off duty. In the bath-house, they relaxed by drinking wine and beer, and gambling with dice.

The toilet at Housesteads Fort could seat sixteen men. They used sponges as toilet paper, washing them in water which flowed through the stone channels.

Roman soldiers once played games with these dice and gaming pieces, found in a fort at Hadrian's Wall.

Many races

The soldiers who served on Hadrian's Wall came from all over the Roman Empire. They included Germans, Spaniards, Africans and Syrians. Although they belonged to many races, they all thought of themselves as Romans. They spoke Latin as well as their own languages. They worshipped the Roman gods, such as Mars, god of war, and Victoria, the goddess who brought victory.

Soldiers' letters

Roman soldiers wrote letters in ink on thin sheets of wood. At a fort called Vindolanda, archaeologists digging in the Roman rubbish found 800 of these letters. They give us a wonderful glimpse of daily life in the fort. In one letter, an officer's wife invites a friend to a birthday party. In another, a soldier begs an officer not to have him beaten with sticks, a common punishment in the Roman army.

Enemies of Roman Britain

The Roman Empire had many enemies. Beyond the frontiers, there were warlike peoples who wanted to get their hands on the Romans' wealth. The Romans called these peoples 'barbarians'.

The Saxons

The greatest threat to the Empire came from the tribes of Germany. In the late 200s, one northern tribe, the Saxons, became pirates. In their long narrow ships, they roamed the seas off Britain and France, capturing merchant ships and raiding the coastal towns.

'They are more brutal than all the others. Entirely at home at sea, they attack without warning. When they are ready to sail home, they drown one in ten of their victims as a sacrifice.'

A Roman writer called Sidonius described the Saxons

The carved head of a monster, from the front of a Saxon ship

The Picts and the Scots

Roman Britain was also raided by two Celtic peoples, the Picts and the Scots. The Picts, meaning 'painted people', lived north of Hadrian's Wall. The Scots lived across the sea in Ireland.

These warriors marching to battle are Picts. Carved stones like this have been found all over eastern Scotland, the homeland of the Picts.

New defences

For many years, the Romans were able to defend Britain from these enemies. They built a chain of forts and watch-towers around the coast. Roman towns were given new strong outer walls.

This fort, at Portchester, was built to keep a watch for the Saxons.

A surprise attack

The worst attack came in AD 367–68, when the Picts, Scots and Saxons joined forces and invaded Roman Britain at the same time. Taken by surprise, the Roman armies were defeated. Towns and country houses were looted. The emperor sent fresh troops to Britain, but it took two years to drive the invaders away.

Roman armies leave Britain

The problem was that the rest of the Roman Empire was also under attack from the German tribes. Eventually, a day came when Rome could spare no more soldiers to defend the Britons. In the early 400s, the Roman armies left Britain for the last time. In AD 410, the Emperor Honorius wrote letters to the leading Britons, telling them that they would have to learn to fight for themselves. From now on, the Britons were on their own.

The coming of the Anglo-Saxons

In the years after AD 400, all the peoples of Germany seemed to be on the move. They swept over the borders of the Roman Empire, raiding, conquering and settling. The tribes who settled in Britain were known as the Angles, Saxons, Jutes and Frisians. Today we call these peoples the Anglo-Saxons, or English.

The Anglo-Saxons were farmers who lived on coastal lowlands. At the time, sea levels were rising and flooding their fields. The Anglo-Saxons had to find another homeland, simply to grow their food.

The routes of the German tribes, as they moved westwards in search of new homelands.

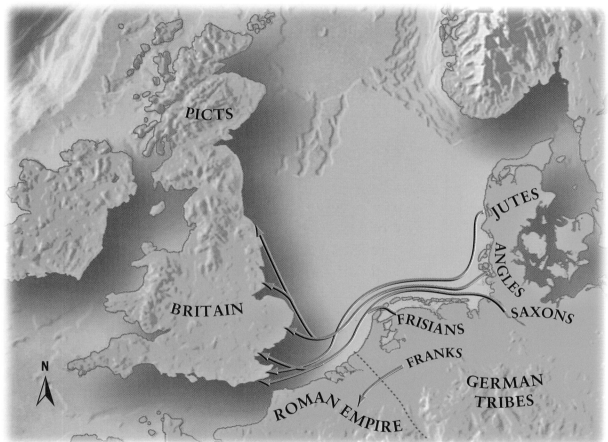

King Arthur, Hengist and Horsa

Hardly any writings from the time have survived. We rely on later stories, told by both Britons and Anglo-Saxons. The Anglo-Saxons remembered two chiefs, called Hengist and Horsa, who were the first to settle in Britain. The Britons told stories about a great war leader called Arthur, who defeated the invaders in battle. But we will never know if these people ever really lived.

Two hundred years of fighting

The Anglo-Saxons found it much harder to conquer Britain than the Romans had done. For more than two hundred years, there was fighting between Britons and Anglo-Saxons. Little by little, the Britons lost their land to the invaders. They were left with kingdoms in the north and west.

The Britons now called themselves by a Celtic name, *Cymry*, meaning 'fellow countrymen'. The Anglo-Saxons had a different name for them. They called the Britons the *Welsh*, which means 'the foreigners'.

Ruined towns

Town life slowly came to an end. People stopped making coins and collecting taxes, and goods were no longer brought to the markets.

Vindolanda fort near Hadrian's Wall. Gradually, all the Roman forts and towns fell into ruin.

'These shattered walls are wonderful to see. The buildings raised by giants are crumbling. The roofs have collapsed, the towers are in ruins, and the builders are long gone, held tightly in the earth's grip.'

A later Anglo-Saxon poem described a ruined Roman town

There was nobody to sweep the streets, which became overgrown with grass and weeds. The Roman buildings began to fall down. People left the towns, to live in the countryside.

The Anglo-Saxons were in awe of the Roman towns. They called the Roman buildings 'the work of the giants'.

Black soil

Archaeologists digging in Roman towns often come across a thick layer of black soil, dating from this time. Black soil, made by rotting plants, shows that the towns had become overgrown with weeds and grass.

Anglo-Saxon settlers

The Anglo-Saxons were farmers, who lived in small villages throughout the countryside. Their houses were made of wood, which quickly rots. But, like Celtic round houses, Anglo-Saxon homes sometimes leave dark marks in the soil where posts once stood. These post holes show us where an Anglo-Saxon farmer once lived.

At West Stow in Suffolk, archaeologists found traces of an early Anglo-Saxon farming village. They have used the evidence to rebuild the houses as they might have looked.

The skeleton of an Anglo-Saxon woman, buried with her bead necklace

Graves

The early Anglo-Saxons did not write books, and their buildings have mostly vanished. Much of what we know about them comes from digging up their graves. Men and women were buried with their most prized possessions. They believed that they could take these with them into the next world.

Warriors were buried with shields, swords and spears. Rich women were buried with jewellery, such as brooches and necklaces. Even the poorest Anglo-Saxons might be buried with goods, such as a joint of meat or a knife.

Place-names

Names on the map show us where the Anglo-Saxons settled. Nine-tenths of English place-names are Anglo-Saxon. You can recognise an Anglo-Saxon place-name by these endings:

bury	= stronghold
den	= valley
ham	= home
ing	= people
ley	= clearing
tun	= village

Place-names often tell us the name of an Anglo-Saxon chief who once lived there. Birmingham, for example, means 'the home of Beorma's people'. Other place-names include the names of Anglo-Saxon gods, such as Woden, god of war. His name can be found in Wednesbury, which means 'Woden's stronghold'.

Britain in AD 600

The Angles and Saxons also gave their names to larger areas of the country. The east and south Saxons gaves their names to Essex and Sussex. The Angles are remembered in East Anglia.

The map shows the four different peoples of Britain in AD 600. The Britons now lived in small kingdoms in the west and north. The Scots from Ireland had set up their own kingdom, called Dalriada, on the coast of what would later be called Scotland. Next to the Scots, there were the Picts. But the south was now in the hands of the Anglo-Saxons.

Each of these peoples had its own language. The Britons spoke Welsh; the Picts spoke another Celtic language, Pictish; the Scots spoke Gaelic, the Celtic language of Ireland; and the Anglo-Saxons spoke English.

Kings and warriors

The Anglo-Saxons were ruled by kings, who each had a following of noble warriors. A good king needed to be skillful in war and very generous. Kings were known as 'ring givers'. They were expected to reward their men with gifts of gold and silver. In return, the warriors were expected to serve loyally. There was no worse disgrace than betraying your lord.

Feasts and poems

When they weren't fighting, the warriors spent their time hunting and feasting. They loved drinking mead, an alcoholic drink made from honey. While they drank, they boasted about their bravery. These drunken boasts were called 'mead speeches'. They also enjoyed poems recited to the music of a harp. Poets made up verses praising generous kings and brave and loyal warriors. Every warrior hoped to be remembered in a poem after his death.

Beowulf

The most famous Anglo-Saxon poem, *Beowulf*, tells the story of a warrior who battles against horrible monsters.

'We all know that we must die one day. A man should win fame before death. That is the best way for a warrior to be remembered.'

The hero of the poem Beowulf *explains why he goes to fight monsters*

The king's purse lid from Sutton Hoo, decorated with strange beasts made from gold, coloured glass and precious stones called garnets.

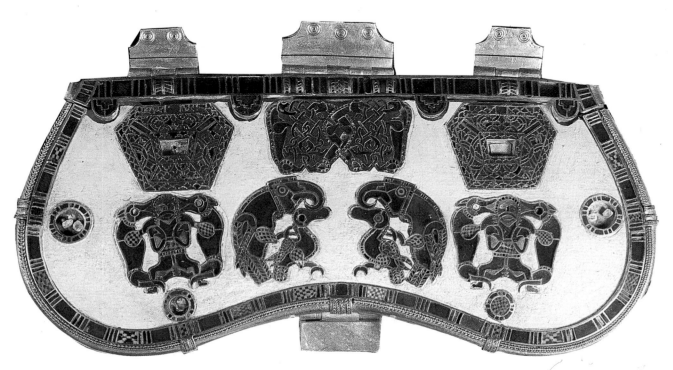

A king buried in a ship

In 1939, archaeologists made a wonderful discovery at Sutton Hoo in Suffolk. Digging into a large mound, they found the remains of a 27 m long ship. Although its planks had rotted away, they had left dark stains in the sand, which could clearly be seen. The ship held the richest treasure ever found in Britain. It included silver bowls, gold coins, beautifully decorated armour, a harp and a set of drinking horns. The ship was the tomb of a king, who died between AD 625 and 640. He was buried with everything he would need in the next world.

The helmet from the royal burial at Sutton Hoo

Beowulf ends with the burial of the hero, killed fighting a huge dragon. Like the king at Sutton Hoo, Beowulf is buried in a mound with treasure.

'Within the mound, they buried rings and jewels. They gave the gold to the earth, and there it still remains. Then twelve brave warriors rode round the mound, sorrowing.'

The description of Beowulf's funeral

This how the king at Sutton Hoo was buried. Once the treasure was in place, a huge mound of earth was piled over the ship.

Christianity

The Christian religion first came to Britain in the late Roman period. After the Anglo-Saxons invaded, the only Christians left were the Britons of the west. In the 400s, Christian Britons took their faith to Ireland. However, they never tried to convert the Anglo-Saxons. The Anglo-Saxons were their enemies. The Britons thought that the less they had to do with them the better.

Columba

In AD 563, an Irishman called Columba sailed to the tiny Scottish island of Iona. He was the leader of a group of Christian holy men, called monks. They built a monastery on Iona, a small group of buildings with a church, where they could live, work, and worship God.

The monastery on Iona was a training place for monks. From Iona, they travelled to other parts of Scotland, preaching their faith and setting up more monasteries. In AD 634, some monks from Iona settled in northern England, building a monastery on the island of Lindisfarne.

Augustine

Meanwhile, another group of monks had arrived in southern England in the year 597. Their leader, Augustine, had been sent from Rome to bring Christianity to the Anglo-Saxons. Augustine soon won over King Ethelbert of Kent. Influenced by their king, many ordinary people joined him in the new faith.

Columba and his fellow Irish monks build their new monastery on Iona

Later monks set up this stone cross on Iona

Other kings followed Ethelbert's example, though some were easier to convert than others. King Redwald of East Anglia agreed to worship Christ, but he carried on praying to his old gods, just in case.

By the year 686, all the rulers of Britain had become Christian. Even so, ordinary people kept the old beliefs for hundreds of years.

Writing

The monks still used the Latin language and the Roman alphabet. This was a great help to Britain's rulers. They now had monks to write laws and letters for them, and to keep records. The monks also began to write down the history of Britain.

New ways of burying the dead

Burial customs changed when people became Christian. Christians believed that God would provide for all their needs in the next world, so there was no point being buried with belongings. Kings were no longer buried in ships stuffed with treasure.

Gods' names

The old gods were no longer worshipped, but they were not completely forgotten. Four days of the week are named after the gods Tiw, Woden, Thunor and Frig. Can you tell which ones?

Monasteries

In the eighth century, there were monasteries all around the British Isles. Many were home to hundreds of monks, and had large areas of land. The monasteries were founded thanks to gifts of land and money from kings and nobles. These founders believed that the monks' prayers would protect them from their enemies, and help them get to heaven when they died.

Life in a monastery

Life was well organised in the monastery. There was an abbot (father) in charge, elected by his fellow monks. One of the monks was called the 'guestmaster'. He looked after the travellers who often came to stay.

The main point of monasteries was worship. At regular times throughout the day and at night, the monks gathered in their church to sing songs praising God. They spent the rest of their time studying, praying, and working in the fields.

In the scriptorium (writing room), some of the monks wrote, copied and illustrated beautiful books. They wrote on the soft skin of calves and sheep, using pens cut from goose feathers. Others were skilled craftsmen, decorating their books with gold and jewels.

A page from a Bible, painted at Lindisfarne monastery around AD 698 by a monk called Eadfrith.

Bede

The most famous Anglo-Saxon writer was a monk called Bede, who lived at the monastery of Jarrow in the early 700s. When he was only seven, his parents handed him over to the monks to be brought up. He wrote a book called *The History of the English Church and People*, in which he described his life.

> 'I have spent all my life in this monastery, and devoted myself to the study of the holy books. And while I have sung daily in church, my chief delight has always been in study, teaching, and writing.'

Bede wrote about his life in the monastery of Jarrow

A group of nuns, led by their abbess, visit an important churchman called a bishop.

Nuns

Women who wanted to lead a religious life became nuns, though there were fewer of them than monks. A nunnery was usually built next to a monastery, with an abbess in charge of both. Abbesses were rich and powerful women, often the daughters of kings. One famous abbess was Hilda, who ruled the monks and nuns of Whitby.

> 'So great was her wisdom that not only ordinary folk, but kings and princes used to come and ask her advice...She was a shining example to all who wished to lead a good life.'

Bede described Abbess Hilda of Whitby

Viking raiders!

For over 150 years, life passed peacefully at the monastery of Lindisfarne, a little island on the coast of Northumbria. The monks spent all their lives praying and working, never dreaming that they might be in danger. Everything changed one day in the year 793, when the monks saw the square sails of ships in the distance. Sea raiders, called Vikings, were coming.

'Never before has such a terror appeared in Britain, nor was it thought possible that such an attack from the sea could be made. See the Church of St Cuthbert spattered with the blood of the priests of God and robbed of all its ornaments!'

Bishop Alcuin of York wrote a letter about the Viking attack on Lindisfarne

A Viking attack

The raiders dragged their ships up on to the beach. Then, waving spears and battle-axes, they rushed towards the monastery. They killed some of the terrified monks, dragging others away to be slaves. After stripping the monastery church of its treasures, they sailed away, disappearing as suddenly as they had arrived.

No-one knew who these raiders were or where they had come from. The raid was shocking, because a monastery was a holy place. Monks could not imagine anyone attacking them, for all the people they knew were Christian. The stormy North Sea was also seen as a barrier against attack. But these raiders had learned to cross this sea in their wooden longships. This meant that they could strike anywhere, at any time.

Who were the Vikings?

The Vikings came from Norway and Denmark, lands known as Scandinavia. They had a lot in common with the earliest Anglo-Saxons. They worshipped the same old gods, under slightly different names. Woden, the war god, they called Odin. They knew Thunor, god of thunder, as Thor. Since they were not Christians, they saw nothing holy about a monastery. To a Viking, a monastery was an undefended place stuffed with treasure. This made it a perfect place to rob.

Vikings in Scotland and Ireland

Soon, Viking ships were appearing all around the British Isles. In AD 795, they attacked Columba's monastery on the Scottish island of Iona. In the same year, they made their first attack on an Irish monastery, on Lambay Island.

The Vikings also began to settle on islands to the north of Scotland. These islands became bases for more Viking raids on Britain and Ireland.

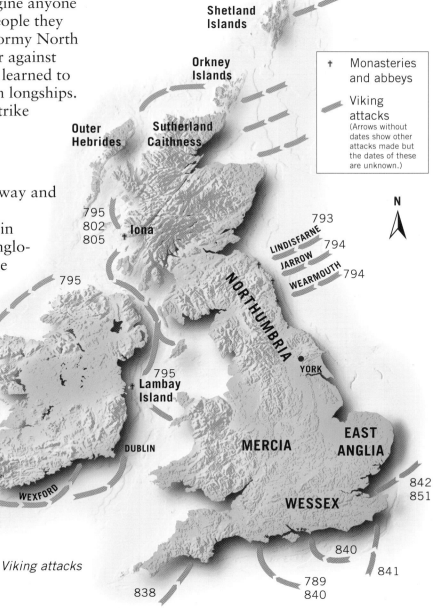

Viking attacks

King Alfred and the Vikings

Viking attacks grew much worse in the 860s. Instead of coming in a few ships, the Vikings began to arrive in huge fleets. Instead of making a quick raid on the coast and sailing away again, they began to make camps, and raid inland.

The Great Army

In 865, a great army of Vikings crossed the sea from Denmark and landed in England. This time, they had come to stay for good. First they conquered Northumbria and killed the king, Aella, as a sacrifice to the god Odin. Then they turned south, overrunning Mercia and East Anglia.

The only kingdom able to fight back was Wessex, in the south west. In one year, 870-71, the Wessex men fought nine battles against the Vikings. Neither side was able to win a total victory. At the end of the year, the Vikings made peace with Alfred, the young king of Wessex.

A lucky escape

In 878, the Vikings made a surprise attack on Alfred's royal hall at Chippenham, where the king was celebrating Christmas. They hoped to capture Alfred and kill him. But he escaped with a small band of warriors, and fled to the marshes of Somerset.

A Viking carving of a longship

The Battle of Edington

For a while, it looked as if the Vikings had conquered the whole of England. But Alfred refused to give up. From his hideout in the marshes, he sent secret messages to the men of Wessex to join him in a new army. In May 878, Alfred met his men and led them to Edington, where the Vikings were waiting.

'Alfred destroyed the Vikings with great slaughter, and chased those who fled to their stronghold, hacking them down. Then he boldly made camp in front of the Viking stronghold with his whole army. Two weeks later, the Vikings, terrified, cold and hungry, asked for peace.'

A monk called Asser described the Battle of Edington

The Danelaw

Alfred made an agreement with Guthrum, the Viking leader. England was split into two areas. Alfred ruled the south-west half, the English kingdom of Wessex. The Vikings were allowed to keep their conquests in the north and east. This area was called the Danelaw, because Danish, rather than English, laws were used there.

Vikings from Norway

Vikings from Denmark

By the year AD 900, Danish Vikings, from the Great Army, had settled in the Danelaw. Meanwhile, other Vikings, from Norway, had settled on the coasts of Scotland, Ireland and western Britain.

Viking settlers

The Vikings were not just fierce warriors. They were also farmers, traders and craftworkers, just like the Anglo-Saxons. The Vikings settled down to farm and to trade in the Danelaw, in Scotland, Ireland and the Isle of Man.

Place-names

Place-names tell us where the Vikings settled in Britain. Viking ones often end in 'by' (a village), 'thorpe' (a tiny village), 'dale' (a valley) and 'toft' (a farm). There are hundreds of these names in the north and east of Britain, but almost none in the south-west. Like Anglo-Saxon place-names, Viking ones often include the name of the man who first settled there. For example, Grimsby, Gaddesby and Kettleby were settled by Vikings called Grim, Gadd and Ketil.

Viking beads found in York (Jorvik)

A Viking brooch found in York (Jorvik)

Jorvik

One of the most important Viking settlements was at York, which the Vikings called Jorvik. (See if you can find Jorvik on the map on page 35.) The town had been founded by the Romans, and, much later, used as a capital by the Anglo-Saxon kings of Northumbria. But Jorvik doubled in size once the Vikings arrived. Merchants from Denmark and Norway sailed up the River Ouse to Jorvik, bringing goods such as slaves, furs and amber, a precious yellow stone. In Jorvik, the craftworkers made beautiful jewellery, including amber necklaces and metal brooches.

The first towns in Ireland

The Vikings built the first towns in Ireland, such as Dublin, Limerick and Cork. They founded these towns on coasts or rivers, places they could easily reach in their ships. Like Jorvik, the Irish towns were great trading centres. All sorts of Irish goods were sent abroad to be sold, but one of the most important trades was in Irish slaves.

Conquering the Danelaw

While the Vikings were settling in the north, King Alfred was turning the towns of Wessex into strongholds, called burhs. He used these as bases to attack the Danelaw. Little by little, the Viking half of England was conquered by Alfred and the kings who followed him. In 937, Alfred's grandson, Athelstan, completed the conquest. He became the first king to rule the whole of England.

This portrait of King Athelstan is the earliest picture of an English king.

Viking words

King Athelstan did not try to drive the Viking settlers out. Most of them had become Christians, and now lived peacefully alongside their Anglo-Saxon neighbours. Many Anglo-Saxons had learned to speak the Viking language as well as English. In time, around 600 Viking words entered the English language. These include:

husband *sky* *knife* *happy* *ugly* *window* *fellow* *egg* *call* *their* *they* *take* *law*

Life on the land

Most British people were not kings or warriors. They were farmers, and changes of ruler hardly affected them. It didn't matter to them whether their king was a Viking, a Celt or an Anglo-Saxon. They had to work just as hard in the fields.

Anglo-Saxon farmers harvesting wheat with sharp scythes

The farmers' life had hardly changed since before the time of the Romans. It was ruled by the seasons. In winter and spring, the farmers ploughed their fields and sowed their wheat, barley or oats. In summer, they cut grass to make hay, to feed their oxen in winter. In August, which the early Anglo-Saxons called 'weed month', people were kept busy weeding the fields. Even the smallest children helped, scaring birds away from the crops.

In the autumn, the sheep were sheared of their wool. Then the whole family worked together, gathering the harvest. When winter came, they took their pigs to the woods to feed on acorns, and started ploughing the fields all over again.

'I go out at daybreak, driving the oxen to the field... I have a lad driving the oxen with a stick, who is now hoarse from the cold and shouting... I have to fill the oxen's bins with hay, and water them, and carry their muck out... It's hard work, because I am not free.'

A farmer describes his work, in a book by a monk called Aelfric

Women's work

Women worked just as hard as the men on the farm. Apart from helping in the fields, they had to milk the cows, and make cheese and butter. They cooked the family meals above a fire on the hearth, in the middle of the house.

Women spin wool by hand and weave cloth on an upright loom. This was daily work for most women.

Women and girls spent a lot of time every day combing wool, to get rid of tangles, and then spinning it into thread. Then they coloured it with dyes they made from plants, and wove it into cloth on a loom.

Runes and riddles

Both the Anglo-Saxons and Vikings used a type of writing called runes. Runes were letters with long upright lines, which made them easy to carve on wood or stone. The Anglo-Saxons had an alphabet of 31 runes, while the Vikings used just 16.

Anglo-Saxon runes

f u th o r c g w   h n i j i/y p x s

t b e m l ng oe d   a ae y ea k k g

Viking runes

f u th o r k   h n i a s   t b m l R

'This is whale's bone. The sea cast up the fish on the rocky shore.'

The runes on the casket (below) explain what the casket is made from

Viking graffiti

On the Scottish island of Orkney, there is an ancient tomb, with stone walls beneath an earth mound. Vikings broke into this tomb, looking for treasure. We know this because the Vikings scratched runes all over the walls. One set reads, 'Ingigerd is the loveliest of women.'

Another tells us why they broke into the tomb: 'Happy the man who can find the great treasure.'

This Anglo-Saxon casket, decorated with runes and pictures, was carved in the early 700s.

Vikings scratched these runes found on a wall in Orkney.

Magic runes

The Anglo-Saxons and the Vikings both believed that runes had magic powers. They could be used to cast spells, to send bad luck to an enemy, or to make someone fall in love with you. If you wore a ring engraved with runes, it would protect you from bad luck. People who knew how to carve magic runes were thought to have great power. They were called 'rune masters'.

The Vikings also carved runes on upright stones, as a way of remembering the dead. Thirty-one such stones have been found on the Isle of Man. A typical carving reads, 'Thorleif set up this stone for Fiac, his son.'

Runes were also used for everyday uses. A sword found in Ireland had 'Dufnall Sealshead owns this sword' scratched on it.

Riddles

The Anglo-Saxons loved riddles. Usually an Anglo-Saxon riddle takes the form of a speech by an everyday object, such as an onion, a book or a key. The object describes itself, and you have to guess what it is. See if you can guess the answer to the riddle on this page. (Turn to page 48 to see if you were right!)

'I come from the cold earth. I was not woven from wool , and neither did silk-worms work to make me. Yet far and wide, I am known as a trustworthy garment for men to wear. You who are clever, speak wisely and say my name is.'

An Anglo-Saxon riddle

The Vikings come back

The years between AD 980 and 1016 were full of trouble for the English. There were more Viking invasions. The new armies were large and well-organized. Unlike the Vikings of King Alfred's time, they did not want to settle in England. They were only after money, and they soon found that the English were willing to give it to them.

Danegeld

King Ethelred of England paid the Vikings huge sums to leave his kingdom. This money, raised from taxes, was called Danegeld (Dane money). Every year, a Viking fleet arrived, burning villages and towns, and asking for the money. Ethelred paid, and the Vikings sailed away. But the payment only made them come back the following year for more.

'The terror caused by the enemy was so great that nobody could think of a plan to get them out of the country, or for holding the land against them.... Despite all the payments, the enemy went about everywhere in bands, robbing and killing our wretched people.'

A monk described the Viking invasions, and the helplessness of the English

Sweyn and Cnut

In 1013, King Sweyn Forkbeard of Denmark brought an even bigger Viking fleet than usual to England. This time, he was after more than just Danegeld. He wanted to be King of England. Ethelred fled to Normandy in France, but Sweyn died before he could be crowned. It was his son Cnut (Canute) who became King of England, in 1016.

Cnut was a strong ruler who brought peace to the kingdom for nineteen years. Each of his two sons then ruled England in turn.

King Cnut and his queen give a new gold cross to the monks of Winchester

The English bring bags and boxes of silver coins to pay off the Vikings.

Edward and the Normans

Meanwhile, Ethelred's son, Edward, was growing up among the Normans, across the sea in France. The Normans were originally Vikings who had settled in France in the early 900s. The name Norman means 'north man', which is what the French called the Vikings.

When Cnut's second son died in 1042, Edward was made King of England. People were pleased to have an Englishman as king again. But Edward must have felt as much Norman as English.

Edward ruled over England for 24 years. When he died, in 1066, there was a new struggle for the throne.

1066

In January 1066, King Edward of England died. He had no sons, and it was not clear who should be king after him. Earl Harold of Wessex, the most powerful English noble, said that Edward had promised him the throne. Duke William of Normandy claimed that he had been made the same promise. Meanwhile, across the sea in Norway, King Harald Hard Ruler also had his eyes on the kingdom.

King Harold

Earl Harold won the backing of the other English nobles, and was crowned on the day of the old king's funeral. He began to plan the defence of his new kingdom. The question was, who would invade first, and where?

Viking invasion

Harald Hard Ruler's Vikings were the first to arrive. In September, they crossed the sea from Norway in a fleet of three hundred longships, invading the north of England. They marched inland and won a great battle against the northern English.

This was bad news for King Harold of England. To make things worse, he

The Norman knights charge towards the English, fighting on foot. This comes from the Bayeux Tapestry, made to celebrate the Norman victory.

learned that his own brother, Tostig, had joined forces with the Vikings and had come to fight against him.

As soon as Harold heard the news, he rushed north with his army. On 25 September, he made a surprise attack on the Vikings, near York, and completely defeated them. Tostig and the Norwegian king were both killed, along with thousands of their men.

The Normans invade

Just three days later, the Normans landed on the coast of Sussex. When Harold heard this terrible news he had to march back south, leading his tired army to fight William.

The Battle of Hastings

The two sides met near Hastings, on 14 October 1066. Unlike the Anglo-Saxons and Vikings, who fought on foot, the Normans had learned to fight on horseback. Harold knew that his best chance was to group his army on a hilltop. The Normans would have a much harder fight if their horses had to charge uphill.

It was a long battle. The English stayed on their hilltop, but they were worn down by the charging horsemen, and by the stream of Norman arrows which filled the air. Towards nightfall, King Harold was killed. William had won.

The last conquest

The Norman conquest was very different from the earlier invasions of the Anglo-Saxons and Vikings. The Normans did not bring large numbers of ordinary people with them. It was an invasion of nobles, not farmers. The old Anglo-Saxon nobles lost their lands to new Norman nobles. But the ordinary English farmers, who made up most of the population, carried on working in their fields.

The Normans were greatly outnumbered by the English. One proof of this is that we still speak English today, not French.

Another proof is the small number of French place-names in Britain.

Castles

At first, the Normans were hated by the English. There were several unsuccessful uprisings against Norman rule. To protect themselves, the Normans built castles throughout the land. Most English people had never seen a castle before 1066 – the English rulers had had no need to build them.

The new Norman castle at Rochester

French words

For the next 300 years, French was the language of the rulers. The English language took on many new French words, especially words to do with law and government. These include advise, judge, rule, command, appeal, royal and parliament.

New names

One big change happened to people's names. Anglo-Saxon and Viking names like Ethelred and Cnut went out of fashion. People began to give their children French names, such as Joan, Alice, Emma, Anne, William, Peter, John and Richard.

William and the Norman kings who followed him, each holding a church he built

Invaders and settlers

The invaders and settlers of the past still affect the way we live. The Celtic languages, Welsh and Gaelic, are still spoken by thousands of people in parts of Wales, Scotland and Ireland. The Romans gave us towns, roads, the alphabet, the calendar and many words. The Anglo-Saxons brought the English language and most English place-names. The Vikings gave us around 600 words and more place-names. Then the Normans arrived, adding French words to our language.

Many peoples

After 1066, there were no more successful invasions of Britain. However, over the years, new settlers continued to arrive. Today, Britain has a very mixed population, with people from all over the world living here. But the country was always home to a mixture of different peoples. Just think of the soldiers from Africa, Spain and Syria who stood guard on Hadrian's Wall, all those years ago.

Published by BBC Educational Publishing
First published 1997
© Peter Chrisp/BBC Educational Publishing 1997
The moral right of the author has been asserted.

Paperback: 0 563 37626 0
Hardback: 0 563 37648 1

Colour reproduction by Daylight Colour Art
Cover origination by Tinsley Robor
Printed and bound by Cambus Litho, Scotland

Illustrations: © Philip Hood 1997 (pages 2–3), © Chris Molan 1997 (pages 28–29, 39), © Ron Tiner 1997 (pages 12–13, 32, 42–43), © Kevin Jones Associates 1997 (pages 8–9)

Photo credits: AKG London **p. 34**; AKG London/© Erich Lessing **pp. 6 (left), 9**; Ancient Art & Architecture Collection/© M & J Lynch **p. 46**; Ancient Art & Architecture Collection/© Ronald Sheridan **pp. 4 (top), 36 (bottom), 41**; Ancient Art & Architecture Collection/© Charles Tait **p. 20 (bottom)**; © Ashmolean Museum, Oxford **p. 24 (bottom)**; Bath Tourism Bureau **p. 17**; Cott Nero D IV f.29 *Lindisfarne Gospels* (c. 698AD) British Library, London/Bridgeman Art Library **p. 30**; *Four Kings of England* by Matthew Paris (1250-59) British Library, London/Bridgeman Art Library **p. 47**; Ms. 298 f.82v *The Presentation of an Abbess* (early 14th century) Fitzwilliam Museum, Cambridge/ Bridgeman Art Library **p. 31**; British Library, London, Cott Aug BV f 6v **p. 38**; British Library, London, Stowe 944 6 **p. 43**; Colchester Museums **pp. 13, 16**; With permission of the Master and Fellows of Corpus Christi College, Cambridge **p. 37**; Dover County Museum **p. 10**; Edinburgh Photographic Library/© Sue Anderson **p. 28**; English Heritage Photographic Library/© Skyscan Balloon Photography **pp. 7, 23 (top)**; English Heritage Photographic Library **pp. 19, 21, 27 (top)**; Exeter City Council **p. 23 (bottom)**; ffotograff/© Charles Aithie **p. 18**; © Michael Holford/British Museum, London **pp. 20 (top), 26, 27 (bottom), 40**; © Michael Holford/Fishbourne Roman Palace **p. 14**; © Michael Holford/Musee de Bayeux **pp. 44, 45**; © Hunting Aerofilms Ltd **p. 15 (top)**; © National Museum of Wales **p. 11**; © Oxford Archaeological Unit **p. 24 (middle)**; Courtesy of Roman Baths Museums, Bath **p. 15 (bottom)**; St. Edmundsbury Borough Council/West Stow Anglo-Saxon Village Trust **p. 24 (top)**; Werner Forman Archive, London **p. 5**; Werner Forman Archive, London/British Museum, London **pp. 4 (bottom), 6 (right)**; York Archaeological Trust **p. 36 (top)**

ANSWER TO RIDDLE ON PAGE 41: The answer is – a warrior's coat of mail! It is made from iron which comes from the 'cold ground'.

Angelina's Best Days Out

Stories by *Katharine Holabird* Illustrations by *Helen Craig*

PUFFIN

To Ben and Vitti, with love   HC

For Tara, Alexandra and Adam   KH

Angelina
at the Fair

Story by *Katharine Holabird* Illustrations by *Helen Craig*

All winter Angelina had been saving her pocket money for the wonderful day when the fair would come again. When she wasn't busy dancing, she would sit by her window and daydream about the big wheel and the roller coaster. She liked all the most exciting rides.

At last, when all the snow had melted and the wind was soft and warm again, the May Day Fair arrived in town. Angelina's ballet class performed a maypole dance at school in celebration of spring, and Angelina almost flew around the maypole she was so excited. All the parents watched and cheered.

After the dance Angelina was ready to go to the fair with her friends, but her parents stopped her. "You've forgotten that little cousin Henry is visiting today," said Angelina's father. "He will be very disappointed if he can't go to the fair with you."

Angelina was furious. "I don't want to take Henry!" she said. "I hate little boys!" But Henry held out his hand just the same, and Angelina had to take him with her. The music from the fair was already floating across the fields and Angelina's friends had gone ahead. She grabbed Henry's hand and dragged him along behind her, running as fast as she could.

At the entrance to the fair was a stand of brightly coloured balloons. "Oh, look!" cried Henry. "Balloons!"

But Angelina didn't pay any attention. "We're going on the big wheel," she said. The big wheel was huge and Henry was frightened, but Angelina loved the feeling of flying up in the air, and so they took two rides.

When they got off Henry felt sick, but he cheered up when he saw the merry-go-round. "Look!" he said. "Can we go on that?"

"Not now," said Angelina. "We're going on the fast rides." She took poor Henry on the roller coaster. Henry shut his eyes and held on tightly as the little car zoomed up and down the tracks. Angelina loved it and wanted to go again, but Henry wasn't sure he wanted to take any more rides at all.

Then Angelina saw the Haunted House.
"I'm sure you'll like this," she said, and pulled
Henry inside.

A big spider dangled just above
their heads as they went in ...

and a skeleton jumped out
and pointed right at them.

When they bumped into a ghost
Angelina reached out to touch Henry …

but he was gone!

"Henry, Henry!" Angelina called, but there was no answer in the darkness. Angelina hurried back through the Haunted House trying to find him.

She looked everywhere until she got tangled up in
the spider and had to be rescued by the ticket seller.

Angelina couldn't see Henry outside the Haunted House either. She ran through the crowds looking for him. She ran past all the rides and all the games, but Henry was nowhere to be found. At last she was so worried and upset that she sat down by the entrance to the fair and began to cry.

And there, watching the balloon man blow up the beautiful balloons, was Henry! Angelina was so relieved that she gave him a big hug and a kiss. "What is your favourite colour, Henry?" she asked. Henry chose a blue balloon.

"What would you like to do now?" Angelina asked kindly.

Henry said he would like to go on the merry-go-round,

so they went on three times and they both loved it.

Afterwards they had a double chocolate ice cream and walked home slowly together. "I like fairs," said Henry, and Angelina smiled.

"You can come with me any time," she said.

Angelina
Star of the Show

Story by **Katharine Holabird** Illustrations by **Helen Craig**

"Welcome on board *The Jolly Rat*, Angelina," said Grandma and Grandpa. "Are you ready to set off for the Mouseland Dance Festival?"

"I can't wait," said Angelina. "I'm going to think up a special dance on the way, so I can be the star of the show! Do you like my costume?"

"It's lovely, but we need all paws on deck to get the boat to the festival," Grandpa reminded her as he started the engine.

But Angelina wasn't listening. She skipped around the deck, imagining her great performance.

"Aren't you going to wear your overalls?" asked Grandma, in surprise. Angelina smiled sweetly and shook her head.

"I've decided to stay in my costume," she said.

As *The Jolly Rat* chugged along through the countryside, Angelina twirled and danced, stopping only to pester her grandparents with questions:

"What do you think of this step?" Angelina asked, and "Does this look nice?"

"You're a sailor now," Grandma reminded her sternly, but Angelina was too busy dancing to be a sailor.

"*The Jolly Rat* needs a new coat of paint,"
Grandpa announced, and he handed
Angelina a paintbrush.

"But Grandpa, I really *have* to practise. I've got a whole new
dance routine to think up!" said Angelina, and she spun
into Grandpa's tin of paint and waltzed off, leaving
little footprints all over the deck!

After that, Grandpa decided Angelina should help Grandma
down in the galley, but Angelina forgot to watch the soup
while she practised pliés and it all boiled over.

That afternoon, Angelina worked on her arabesques and it wasn't long before she got all tangled up in Grandma's washing and Grandpa's fishing line. She had to be rescued by both her grandparents, who were getting very grumpy. "That's enough, Angelina!" they cried.

When Angelina went
to bed that night, she promised
Grandma and Grandpa that she would
stop dancing, but the very next morning she forgot,
and performed a magnificent series of leaps along the deck.

The deck was slippery and Angelina lost her balance.
She tumbled right into a can of oil and
got covered from head to toe in
horrible black grease.

"Oh no – look what I've done!"
Angelina gasped. Her beautiful costume was ruined.

Angelina was so horrified that she raced below deck to her bunk bed and cried her heart out. Then, just when she had decided she was the worst mouseling in the world, Grandma came to give her a cuddle.

"I'm sorry, Grandma!" Angelina sobbed. "I haven't been very helpful, have I?"

"I know you're sorry," said Grandma, as she dried Angelina's tears.

"I haven't got anything to wear to the dance festival now," sniffed Angelina. "And I can't do my dance without a costume!"

"Well, let's see what's in my old chest," suggested Grandma. And there, inside the chest, they found a beautiful sailor suit.

"That was my favourite outfit," Grandma said, "and that's me wearing it," she added proudly, pointing to a faded photograph that was hanging on the wall.

"Ooh," gasped Angelina excitedly. "Do you think I could borrow it if I'm very careful?"

"Of course," smiled Grandma, "I'll add some special ribbons."

For the rest of the journey, Angelina wore her old overalls, and she tried very hard to be a real sailor.

Before long, she could steer *The Jolly Rat* down the Mousetail Canal.

She swabbed the decks and painted the woodwork with Grandpa, and she cooked with Grandma down in the galley.

She even baked her grandparents some Cheddar cheese pies!

And in the evenings after supper, while Grandpa played his penny whistle, Grandma showed Angelina some of her favourite dances.

"Thank you, Grandma," said Angelina one night, "you've given me a wonderful idea."

A few days later, *The Jolly Rat* arrived at the Mouseland Dance Festival with a new coat of paint and all decked out in garlands of flowers.

Angelina proudly tooted the horn.
"We're here!" she shouted.

As the festival opened, Grandpa played his penny whistle and Angelina performed her new dance. It was a special sailor's jig that she'd practised with Grandma. The crowds loved the show and cheered for more.

"Hooray for the little sailor!" they shouted.

MOUSELAND
DANCE
FESTIVAL

When the evening was over, Angelina hugged her grandparents.

"You really were the star of the show," said Grandma.

"And you're the very best Grandma and Grandpa in the whole of Mouseland!" Angelina replied.

Then they all joined paws and skipped happily back to *The Jolly Rat*.